David Morgan

The Family Store

David Morgan

The Family Store

AN ILLUSTRATED HISTORY 1879-2005

by Brian Lee

breedon **books**
PUBLISHING

First published in Great Britain in 2005 by
The Breedon Books Publishing Company Limited
Breedon House, 3 The Parker Centre, Derby, DE21 4SZ.

Dedication
To my wife, Jacqueline Lee, and all those who shopped and worked at David Morgan Ltd.

ISBN 1 85983 452 3

Printed and bound by Cromwell Press, Trowbridge, Wiltshire.

Contents

Author's Acknowledgements

First of all I would like to thank John Morgan for asking me to compile this book and for allowing me to have access to the store's archives. I also need to thank the Lord Lieutenant of South Glamorgan, Captain Norman Lloyd-Edwards GC. StJ, RD, JP, RNR, for writing the foreword.

Special thanks go to James Shaughnessy and Mike Thomas of David Morgan Ltd for their valued assistance. Others I need to thank are Beatty French for loaning me her photograph album and freelance photographers Roy Paul and Glyn Paul of Press & Commercial Photographers, Llanmaes Street, Grangetown, Cardiff, for supplying me with pictures taken on the final shopping day in the store.

I am also indebted to those people who answered my requests for photographs in the local press. My appreciation also to Tony Woolway, chief librarian at the *Western Mail & Echo,* for his help. Finally, my thanks to all at Breedon Books for publishing this book at the shortest of notice and for getting it on the bookshelves within a few months of the store closing.

brian@thepress.fsnet.co.uk

Foreword

This year, 2005, Cardiff celebrates 100 years of being made a city and 50 years since being declared the capital city of Wales. Although there is great rejoicing there is also a tinge of sadness as one of Cardiff's most revered institutions is no longer with us. For after 125 years, David Morgan, the store which offered a complete family service – and run by a family – has gone the way of those other family stores: Marments, Evan Roberts and Seccombes.

The Morgans and their immediate successors fully appreciated the massive potential of Cardiff and were determined to use their entrepreneurial skills to further develop their businesses. When the news that David Morgan was to close broke, there was a sense of disbelief bordering on grief among thousands of people in Cardiff and the Valleys to whom the store had meant so much throughout their lives.

My earliest recollection was as a very small boy being brought from Merthyr with my mother on shopping expeditions (my father wisely stayed at home), but most memorably, once a year, coming to the pantomime at the New Theatre. This was always preceded by a visit to Father Christmas in the store's grotto and then a sumptuous lunch in the Oak Room.

The restaurant seemed enormous to a small boy but being there was an essential part of the Christmas holiday. I never thought then that some 36 years later I would be in that same room (it seemed much smaller then) attending a dinner to mark the store's centenary. We all went home with a commemorative glass tumbler and a paperweight embossed with the entry made by the founder in his ledger book on 31 October 1879, stating that he had opened the shop that day.

Shopping in David Morgan's was a social occasion when everyone wore their best clothes. Chairs were provided at the counters for the customers while the shop walker (another historic term) ensured that the customer was promptly attended by the ever-courteous staff.

In 1993 the North Atrium was completed with escalators to each floor, and I was invited to perform the opening ceremony. A memorable occasion not least because, having been assured by John Morgan that this would be a very low key affair, I arrived on the appointed evening to find 120 people sitting in chairs awaiting a fairly formal speech, which I had to deliver in the lingerie department. While various photographs were being taken I was only too conscious of the background of some provocative clothing, including a red basque. Fortunately I escaped with my reputation reasonably unscathed!

It has been my enormous pleasure over the years not only to be a customer of the store but to know many of the family who were involved in its running. I think fondly of Trevil and Gerald who were such characters in their own right in the life of Cardiff and of course my contemporaries, brothers John and Richard, who have managed the business since their uncles died, and David, a London solicitor, the non-executive chairman.

The closure must have been a very sad time for them, ending such a long family tradition, but they have left with the heartfelt appreciation of thousands of people who looked upon the store as part of their family as well as the Morgans.

This book is a fitting tribute to one of South Wales's most distinguished and respected patriarchies and one which will bring back very many fond memories.

Captain Norman Lloyd-Edwards, GC. StJ, RD, JP, RNR
Lord Lieutenant of South Glamorgan

The Morgan Family

The slogan 'The Family Store' means different things to different people. It originally meant that the store was owned and managed by the Morgan family. Except for the last few years, the senior directors have been drawn from four generations of Morgans, an unusual achievement by any standard.

The dominant figure throughout has been the man with his name over the door, the founder, David Morgan. His trading policies and concern for his staff have been articles of faith followed by his successors. A draper by trade, he disliked furniture because the messy straw in which it was packed was brought onto the shop floor. This did not stop his son, John Llewellyn, 'Jack', building the handsome North Building, completed in 1912, to house the new furnishing departments. David Morgan went to his business regularly, up until the end of his long life when he died in 1919 at the ripe old age of 86. Jack was responsible, in 1929, for building between the two previously separate shops, the original in The Hayes and the second in St Mary Street, to form one store.

Bernard, Jack's eldest son, joined the business in 1925 after serving in World War One, university and a fact-finding tour in the US. He was a man of his time because his skill with figures and strong financial control probably saved the business during the depression of the thirties and World War Two in the forties. His brother, Aubrey, was in the business for a short time before going to America for personal reasons. In the pre-war years the third brother, Trevil, mixed shopkeeping with playing cricket for Glamorgan while Gerard, the youngest, was at university. In 1945, after war service, Trevil and Gerald returned to the business. Just as post- war shortages were ending and happy days were here again, Bernard died unexpectedly, in 1955, aged 56. Trevil became managing director and was the merchant in charge of the 'front of the house', while Gerald was the administrator and managed the arcade properties. They saw steady growth and consolidation during these years of great social change and bought a branch in Penarth in 1959.

Bernard's sons, John and Richard, started working for David Morgan in 1959 and 1960, as soon as they were available after national service and university. After training in larger stores in England, they both did a series of jobs as they gained experience, John concentrating on merchandising and Richard on administration and finance.

When Gerald died in 1974 and Trevil in 1976, it was natural that John should step into Trevil's shoes and Richard into Gerald's. This happy arrangement saw many years of development and even heady achievement. Fallow space on upper floors, originally built for 'living in', was brought into service by a comprehensive network of escalators.

After the acquistion and development of property in Bakers Row, the Hayes end of the store was enlarged to the extent that the St Mary Street end became redundant; the space vacated was added to let properties in the Royal and Morgan Arcades.

Over the years, other members of the family contributed to the business in key roles. During World War Two, Trevil's wife gave invaluable help to her brother-in-law, and his daughter, Elisabeth, was display manager in the fifties. John's sister, Eleanor, was a buyer in the sixties, his wife managed the Penarth store in the eighties and his daughter, Ann Mary, was catering manager for a short time in the early nineties.

After John and Richard retired at the end of the nineties, the store sadly lost momentum under non-family management. This, together with the problems of trading in such old buildings and the threat of large new retail developments nearby, meant that, in spite of the company's strong financial position, sale of the building for redevelopment and closure was the only realistic option. Now, the Founder would not have recogised the inside of his store, but would have cherished the spirit and camaraderie of the staff, the greater Family, which was maintained until the doors were closed for the last time.

John Morgan

David and William Morgan in 1918. This was the last photograph of David Morgan, who died on 19 April 1919. The photograph was taken at William's farm near Brecon.

A family group photograph taken at Southerndown on 30 April 1924. Front row, left to right: Messrs William Hall, James Hall, J. Llewellyn Morgan, and David Hall. Back row, left to right: Messrs John Hall, A.J. Morgan, D.B. Morgan, J. Trevil Morgan and Thomas Hall. The Halls and A.J. Morgan were first cousins of Bernard and Trevil Morgan.

This delightful family picture was taken on the 40th wedding anniversary of John Morgan's grandparents at the family home in Fairwater Road, Llandaff, Cardiff, on 17 August 1938.

John Watkeys Morgan entered the business in 1880 and almost completed 75 years with the company in every capacity up to director. Like David Morgan he was from Breconshire but was not a relation. The portrait of him is now with his family. His nephew stands in front of the portrait, photographed on 31 October 1993.

The brothers John Morgan, Richard Morgan and David Morgan.

John Morgan with his mother, Mary Morgan, and daughter, Ann Mary.

Introduction

When David Morgan opened his store on The Hayes on 31 October 1879 he couldn't have had any idea that what was once a little draper's shop would become one of the city's best loved landmarks and an institution in itself.

The centre of Cardiff, in those days, was cluttered with some 45 courts and these included Green Garden Court, Evan Court, Kingstone Court and Dalton Court. Some were neat and clean while others were squalid, and it is little wonder that brothels and shebeens flourished in the area.

Some years ago, when the David Morgan clock was taken down for repairs, the store was inundated with telephone calls and letters asking what had happened to it. So imagine the sadness most Cardiffians feel now that the store is just a memory.

Here are just a few of those memories. Graham Gaskin, whose father William worked as a Morgan Arcade inspector for more than 35 years, told the *South Wales Echo*: '*My parents, three sisters and one brother all moved into a flat at the St Mary Street end of the arcade. A climb of 70 stairs was required to reach our home in the sky and although often cursed, was very good exercise. I was born there in 1933. I well remember the early 1940s during the air raids, running along the arcade towards The Hayes with my mother and three sisters accompanied by the sounds of the guns and bombs falling. Often the shrapnel from the shells pierced the glass roof of the arcade, falling around us. It was wonderful to reach the safety of the David Morgan basement air-raid shelter. This was situated where the furniture and bedding departments are now.*'

Joyce Herbert and her two daughters, Karen and Lynne, all share special memories of the store. Herbert was the first member of the family to purchase her dress for her wedding to Mervyn from David Morgan and she told the *Echo*: '*In March 1961 I was getting married and purchased my wedding dress and material for my bridesmaids' dresses and also my going away suit from David Morgan. In July 1997 our eldest daughter Karen was getting married, she also bought her wedding dress and bridesmaid dresses from David Morgan. In July 1999 our youngest daughter Lynne was getting married, she also purchased her wedding dresses and bridesmaid dresses from the store. So you can guess I have very fond memories of this store.*'

Mary McAleavey, who joined the staff of David Morgan when she was just 14, has been living with a David Morgan secret for more than 60 years. She told the *Western Mail*: '*Staff had to clock in and I recall, one day in 1942, my friend Nellie Lewis came to work and found that her pet dog, Chum, had followed her from home. She had no time to go back home so we decided to hide the dog in the staff washroom so as the department managers, Jack and Jenny Broughton, wouldn't find out. After what seemed like an eternity, lunch arrived and we went to take Chum home, but to our horror we discovered that he had ruined the beautiful flooring and walls in his efforts to get out.*' A distraught Lewis took her pet home convinced that she would be sacked, but later Broughton appeared and told her not to use the washroom as there were rats in there. Nobody told on Nellie, and the staff were in fits of laughter when the pest control people were brought in.

The Golden Girls, as they were called, met in the store's restaurant on the first Friday of every month for the past 15 years. They were all members of Moorland Road Primary School, Cardiff, and after meeting up at a school reunion made David Morgan Ltd their headquarters.

Tales of ghosts, suicides and romance in the store are all there for the telling. However, now is the time for the following images to do the 'talking'.

The Early Days

David Morgan in the Tabernacle burial grounds, The Hayes, in August 1902. The cemetery was eventually cemented over.

David Morgan's son, John Llewellyn Morgan, posed for this picture on 14 May 1898.

These workers used pick axes to clear the site of the works department *c*.1902. The building behind the workers is the rear of the optician in the Royal Arcade, owned for many years by Percy Randle.

A worker is seen standing in the corner of the Tabernacle burial grounds, almost at the same spot as Morgan on page 13.

The buildings at the rear of St Mary Street was where Anderson & Co were situated.

Anderson & Co, on St Mary Street, who advertised themselves as 'the cheapest clothiers in the world', *c*.1890.

This was Kingston Court in 1902. It was situated between the Royal Arcade and Brains' Brewery. In the background of the top picture the top of the Royal Hotel can be seen.

Some 45 courts containing 327 houses were built in the centre of Cardiff during its rapid growth in the second half of the 19th century.

Rising Sun Court. The middle building is in the background. The site was cleared and used as the winter quarters of Studt's travelling circus before the north building was built in 1912.

A photograph of Green Garden Court. The open doorway in the top picture led to Tabernacle Lane, *c.*1928. Compere the picture with the one on page 101 (bottom) for a before and after.

Golden Lion Court, now known as
Bakers Row, was off Wharton Street.
This picture was taken on 5 July 1897
by Wills the Photographers, for
David Morgan.

Kingston Court was one of the tidier ones, as can be seen in this picture, *c.*1902.

Morgan & Company, Nos 23 & 24 The Hayes, after the first addition to the store in 1880.

The Royal Arcade is to the extreme left of the picture, *c.*1902.

Morgan & Company on St Mary Street. Watkeys Morgan is the second from the left on the picture, *c.*1891.

The Pavilion public house can be seen to the right of both pictures (above and right). It was formerly The Duke of Cornwall, which was bought by David Morgan at the turn of the century.

The staff posed for this picture outside No. 28 Morgan & Company, The Hayes, *c.*1900.

The tram lines tell us that this picture of Morgan & Company was taken after the first electric tram cars came to Cardiff in 1902. It was taken in 1904 on completion of the façade (except the 1912 north building).

The David Morgan shop on St Mary Street was decorated for the Queen's coronation in 1953.

The David Morgan building on The Hayes during the 1960s.

The well-known David Morgan clock is taken
down for repairs.

The clock had been a familiar landmark for
generations of Cardiffians. The original clock,
made by Gillet & Johnston of Croydon, was
erected in 1904. By 1986 it had rusted beyond
repair, but Gillet & Johnston still had the original
drawings and were able to make an exact copy
from fibreglass.

David Morgan by day in May 1978.

David Morgan by night in December 1957.

Transport

A three-year-old Ford van. The name here is Morgan & Co as the store did not become a limited company until 1916.

A David Morgan Elite van, which must date from after 1916 as it now reads David Morgan Limited.

A David Morgan Commer van. The bodywork was done by W. Lewis & Sons of Tudor Lane, Cardiff, *c*.1930.

Osbourne Long, Portrait and Commercial photographers of Queen Street, Cardiff, took this picture of these proud David Morgan drivers, *c*.1930.

All these David Morgan van drivers wore either caps or trilbys when they posed for this picture.

Unlike the top picture, all the vans faced the camera for this photograph, *c.*1930.

A David Morgan van, *c.*1933.

A David Morgan van, *c.*1938. These vans were parked in Llandaff overnight during the war to avoid the Blitz.

These four pictures show the evolution of the David Morgan van, photographed in *c.*1950, *c.*1958, *c.*1964 and *c.*1961 respectively.

Promotions and Displays

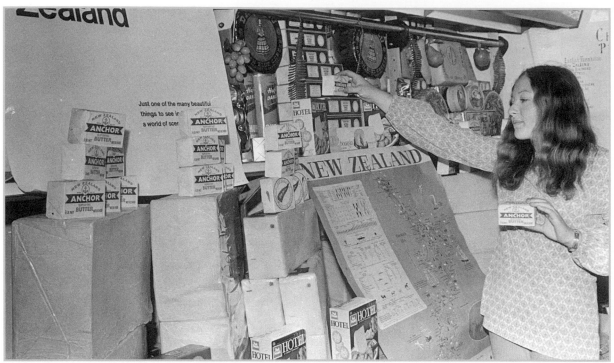

A David Morgan display artist arranges a display of New Zealand butter and cheese in the food hall for a 'New Zealand fortnight' promotion, *c.*1976.

Sylvia Beale of Rhiwbina, Cardiff, selects a jar of New Zealand honey, helped by her four-year-old daughter, Sonia.

Helena Rubinstein holiday and beauty festival and lingeric display, *c.*1971.

This 'Travel in Tricel with Ford' display, *c.*1971, used fashions, travel goods and accessories from David Morgan.

A Dairy Crest Welsh butter promotion in 1964.

Ambrosia milk puddings were on offer for just 10p in 1964.

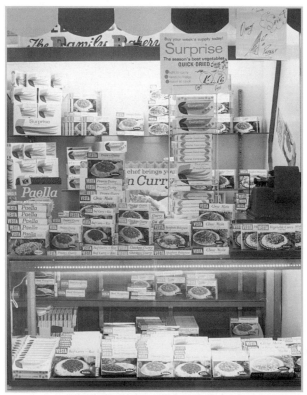

Before takeaways became popular, many people made do with Vesta chicken and beef curry products, *c*.1964.

Mary Baker cake mixes were all the rage in 1964.

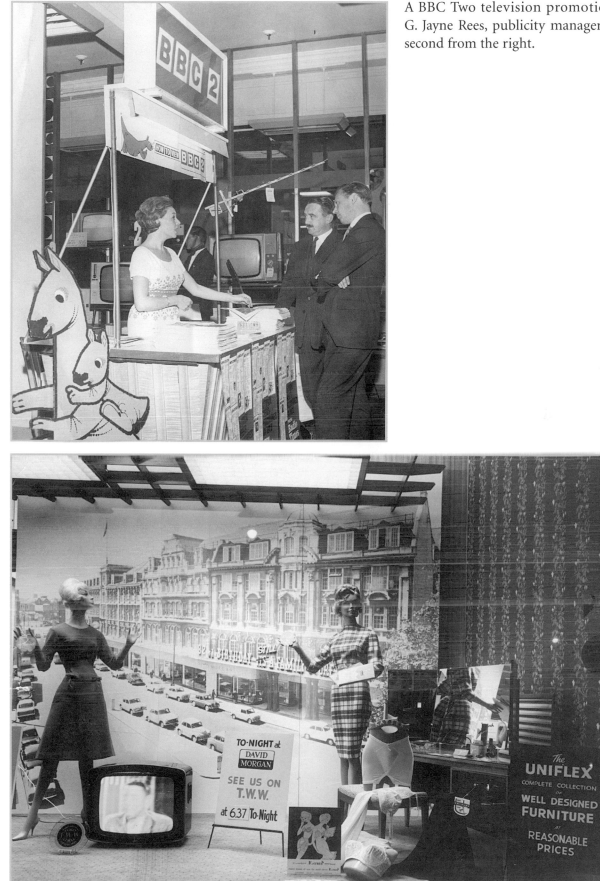

A BBC Two television promotion. G. Jayne Rees, publicity manager, is second from the right.

In 1961 David Morgan advertised their store on *Television Wales and the West*.

The gentleman wearing spectacles is Gerry Kingston and his *Western Mail & Echo* colleague, standing next to the photographer, is Johnny Mansell. But who is the celebrity they have come to see?

This lucky little unknown boy, possibly now in his late forties, got to sit on the celebrity's lap.

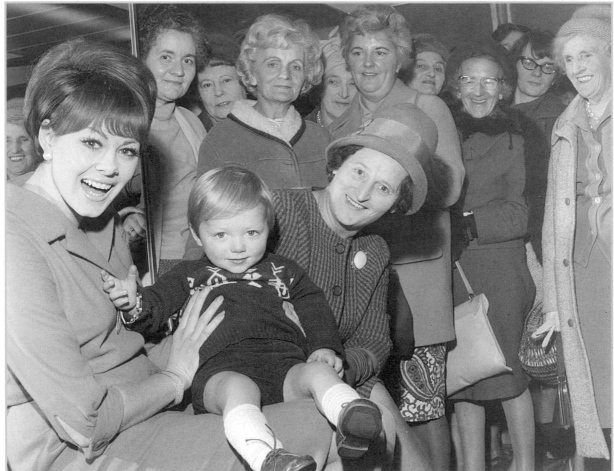

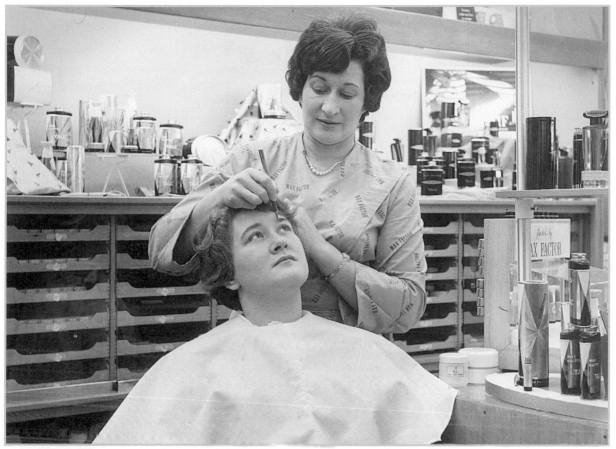

This young lady is being made up by a Max Factor make-up specialist, *c*.1960.

A Kayser promotion within the store in 1960. Pamela Andrews (Kayser Lingerie Princess), pictured first left, and Mary Thomas (Hosiery Princess) chat with Miss Davies, who was known as Dell.

This refrigerator cost £56 14s in 1961, as part of an Electrolux promotion.

A 'Wales in the world of sport' exhibition was staged in 1958, the year the Empire & Commonwealth Games came to Cardiff.

David Morgan supplied the uniform worn by the Welsh team at the 1954 British Empire & Commonwealth Games, held in Vancouver.

Peerless Jim Driscoll, Jimmy Wilde, Tommy Farr, Joe Erskine and Phil Edwards are just some of the famous Welsh boxers depicted in this exhibition.

Window Displays

The Redia underwear window display at The Hayes. The reflection of the British Volunteer hotel can be seen in the top of the picture, *c.*1926.

The price of the ladies' coat on the left of the picture is seven guineas or seven pounds and seven shillings, photographed in 1967. This is the corner of the Royal Arcade and Tabernacle Lane.

These coats were all the rage in the 1960s. Note the opening hours; the store was closed on Mondays. Those were the days.

A summer dress display in 1966.

Cotton dresses 'as seen in Vogue' in 1962.

Dacton 'in Vogue' dresses in 1962.

In 1966 all the bathing costumes in this Hayes window display were under £2.

The nightie on the extreme left cost 65 shillings (£3.25), c.1960.

The 'you feel so good in wool' display in 1964.

There is certainly an art to window dressing, as these two pictures from the 1960s suggest.

The 'British fashion is wonderful in crimplene' display, *c.*1969.

The 'Croeso 69' display.

This dining room set would have cost you £197 7s 6d in 1956.

'And who lives in a house like this?' A furniture window display, c.1965.

A 'kitchen of today' display, *c.*1950.

A 'modern kitchen' display in 1960.

A fairly modern bedroom display from 1951.

A display of Schimmelpenninck, Holland's finest cigars, in 1966.

The 'temptation boutique' display in September 1979.

Christmas Time

No doubt this little boy and his sister had what they wanted for Christmas, *c*.1960.

Jeanne Fenton and her brother Andrew, from Penarth, in Santa's grotto in 1984.

It was just two shillings (10p) to have a postcard-sized photograph taken with Father Christmas in the 1950s as advertised on the ceiling, right.

There was a large display of toy soldiers in 1959.

The entrance to the 'stairway to storyland' bazaar in 1953.

The 'Father Christmas telephone service' in 1953. It was just threepence to phone Santa.

Cowboy outfits seemed to be in vogue when this picture was taken in 1959.

Meccano sets, Robin Hood costumes and post office sets were just some of the goodies on sale in 1959.

In the 1930s, rocking horses were obviously a great favourite with the children.

The adults appear to be just as
fascinated with these Mettoy toys
as the children, c.1936.

Father Christmas and his Toyland staff pose for this picture outside the 'Jack and Jill' bazaar.

All these dolls on display and not a Barbie among them.

VISIT
TOY
LAND

JACK &

OLD WOMAN'S SHOE

1912

FURNISHERS

BAGS &
TRUNKS

Handbags

This illuminated 'old woman's shoe' display sign must
have captivated hundreds of children on their way to
the Christmas bazaar.

The 'old woman's shoe' exhibit. Note the well hole in the north building. This was floored over after 1945.

This was the scene inside the 'old woman's shoe' exhibit.

'Oh You Beautiful Doll.' A display from the Christmas Bazaar in 1931 and still not a Barbie in sight.

Entrance to the Toyland 'Peter Pan' grotto, c.1960.

The Dr Who Dalek, left of picture, confirms that this photograph was taken in the 1960s.

This was the entrance to Ali Baba's cave in 1951.

Bicycles and toy cars were in demand in 1953.

Puss in Boots
helps Santa with
the children,
*c.*1960.

This little Red Indian is wearing the latest fashion spectacles.

The 'enchanted castle' and 'the pageant of fairy tales' were the themes of this Christmas bazaar, *c.*1960.

Penny Jenkins receives a Christmas present from Father Christmas. She later worked part-time in the store before starting her nursing career, c.1961.

A brother and sister, Gareth and Claire Hurford, aged seven and five, with Father Christmas in 1971.

Staff at David Morgan pose for a Christmas photograph in 1994. It was for a Christmas card to send to account customers and to celebrate the opening of the north atrium.

City Hall Centenary Ball

The City Hall Ball was on 6 October and staff were invited to a 'Victorian Evening'.

In 1979 David Morgan Ltd celebrated its centenary. Dressed in Victorian costume are, left to right: Pauline Horsey, Roy Bullen, Ken Jermyn and Alan Horsey (director).

John Morgan and his wife Doreen are at the right of the picture. The gentleman on the extreme left is Mr Morgan's brother, Richard, with Carol Hooper. Deborah Haig and Elizabeth Richards are in the centre.

John and Doreen Morgan.

'Please raise your glasses ladies.' Left to right:
Janice Davies, Sandra Porter, Hilary Payne,
Kitty Rayner and Gladys Provan.

'The order of the garter.' Left to right: Nina Jones, Maisie Brown, Tina Boughton, John Tennant (toy buyer), Cynthia Blick, name unknown.

Among this crowd are Joyce Harries, Elizabeth Richards and Nancy Edwards.

'Some chaps get all the luck'. Gloria Thornburn and Debbie.

'I'll drink to that,' say Helen Williams and Faye Rowe.

Such style and eloquence. Left to right: Margaret Goodwin, Audrey Perkins, Doris Fenton and Kathleen Taylor.

Janice Davies and Kitty Raynor: 'Do you see who I see?'

These cleaning ladies had a ball.

Ken Smithers, David Price, Dolores Rich and Zena Lucas.

Some Famous Faces

The Barron Knights pop group visited the store on 27 November 1968.

An alarmed-looking 'Butch' of the Barron Knights.

These three members of the Barron Knights are busily signing autographs for their fans.

On this occasion in the October of 1962, singer Michael Holliday gets all the attention. Sadly, just over 12 months later, he died of a suspected drugs overdose.

Seen left of the picture is Ken Jones, the legendary Welsh rugby player and Olympic sprinter. He had the honour of handing the Queen's message to her husband, the Duke of Edinburgh, at the opening of the 1958 Empire & Commonwealth Games in Cardiff.

Olympic long jump gold medallist Lynn Davies and his wife, Meriel, choose some material while the American long jump world record holder, Ralph Boston, looks on in 1965.

Television personality Christine Godwin and her husband, Glamorgan County cricketer Ossie Wheatley, with David Morgan competition winners, c.1977.

The Secretary of State for Wales, Peter Walker, unveils a plaque commemorating the opening of the new Atrium. With him is managing director John Morgan on 19 September 1988. The logo of Turners, who were the builders, can be seen in the reflection on the plaque.

The world famous opera singer Sir Geraint Evans cuts the ribbon at the opening of the new escalator. Managing director John Morgan lends a hand and his elder brother, David, is on the right. This was the centenary night on 31 October 1979.

Designer Laurence Llewelyn-Bowen posing for a picture in the store with two pretty young ladies in 2000.

HTV's Arfon Haines Davies with staff member Beatty French in 2004.

Spoon bender Uri Geller was up to his old tricks again when he visited the store in 2000.

Television star Michael Aspel, who worked as an assistant in the store in the 1950s, pays a final visit to the store in 2004.

Richard Morgan with Michael Aspel.

Welsh singer Peter Karrie at the January sales in 2005.

The left picture shows BBC Wales' Nick Patel with Beatty French and right with Mags O'Keefe.

Behind the Scenes

The Counting House was situated on the first floor of the middle building, later becoming the linen department. Sumlock comptometres were introduced to Great Britain in around 1926.

Mary Hamilton operating the logabox sales dissection machine, c.1960.

Telephone operators Janet Spear and Ruth Watts, *c.*1950.

The gentleman on the phone to the right of the picture is Mr Smears, *c.*1950.

A girls' best friend, so they said, was a sewing machine. Above are Mary Wheeler and Lilian Roblin and below are Pat Jones and R. Legge, c.1950.

Cabinet maker and French polisher Maurice Pritchard worked in the store for 47 years.

Margaret Stott in the publicity department, c.1955.

TV engineer Mr Walker services early televisions, c.1955.

The staff office was situated on the second floor at the rear of the middle building, *c*.1955.

Carpet fitters Dave Piper and Alf Mumin in 1960, before broadloom carpet became popular.

The Counting House, before conversion to the sports department, in December 1976.

A bookbinding demonstration, held in the store in 1964.

Chef Tom Singer slices a joint of ham, *c*.1955.

The restaurant's Japanese Room, c.1930. In recent years this was the Wedgwood department.

The restaurant's Georgian Room, looking towards the Japanese Room, c.1930. This became the Royal Mint and Worcester China departments.

Waitress Laura Da Cruz is seen serving Ruth Watts and Hilda Morgan, *c*.1955.

The waitress could be saying, 'That comes to seven shillings and sixpence.' This is the same room that is pictured at the top of page 91.

Various Departments

Some older shoppers may remember the post office in the store, which was situated on the first floor of the middle building and more recently became the ladies fashion department. This picture was taken in 1948.

The despatch department in the basement. Fred King (right) was despatch manager, pictured with Messrs Lavery and Daly.

The *Hotspur* and *Bonanza* annuals were on sale at the cash desk in the store in December 1965.

One could even book a London theatre ticket in the store, *c.*1960.

The ladies in the picture are Paula Haines, Carol Fry and Dilys Edwards, c.1960. This is the curtain fabrics department on the first floor.

This is the dress fabrics department on the ground floor of the St Mary Street building (vacated by the store in 1993), and the assistant serving the customer is Pat Ray, c.1960.

An assistant lends a helping hand, c.1960.

Window dressers at work, c.1960.

Assistant Harry Simmonds gets Davies to try on some raincoats, c.1960.

Harry Simmonds tries on a coat for size and is helped by David Newberry, c.1960.

The Food Hall, situated in The Hayes building on the ground floor, was originally installed in 1959 and refitted in 1975.

With Fairy Snow, Tide, Daz, Persil and Omo brands of washing powder on sale, housewives had plenty of choice, c.1966.

The linen department on the first floor of the middle building in 1977. This light well was used to install the middle building escalators.

Cut price toiletries in 1977.

The new perfumery department in the middle building in September 1979.

The children's department on the ground floor of St Mary Street in 1977. Assistant Marion Morgan is on the right of the picture.

Everything for the dressmaker could be found on the ground floor, photographed in 1960.

The ladies coats department in 1960.

Pots, pans, pails and even rose trees could be purchased in this department stent, photographed in 1960. This is the south basement. Compare it with the picture on the bottom of page 107.

Material was sold by the yard when the top picture was taken in 1948 and by the metre when the bottom picture was taken of the same department 30 years on, in 1977.

The Menswear department in 1957, on the middle ground floor.

The sports department on the second floor of Green Garden Court; a new venture started in 1977. Compare it with the photograph at the top of page 89.

The rear of the coat department on the first floor of The Hayes building, before the installation of the fur salon, in December 1976.

The fur salon on the first floor of The Hayes building was opened in September 1977.

The beds were on the first floor of the middle building, before the carpet department was moved up to make room for Miss Selfridge, in December 1976.

The 'clock room' was situated on the second floor of the middle building, photographed in December 1976. It was so called because the controls for the clock on the Hayes façade were in the floor.

The gift department on the second floor of The Hayes building, which replaced the original hair salon in 1977. See photograph at the top of page 109.

The china basement in The Hayes building was installed in 1971. This picture was taken in the summer of 1977. See photograph at the bottom of page 102.

The surnames of the assistants are believed to be Tapper and German but the bride is unknown, c.1960.

The bridal salon on the first floor of The Hayes building was completed in December 1978 and this picture was taken in September 1979.

This picture of the French of London hair salon was taken in December 1976, before its demolition and conversion of the area to the gift department. Contrast this with the picture at the top of page 107.

The 'clock room' on the second floor of the middle building, before installation of accounts desks in 1976.

The windows at the rear of this picture faced on to Morgan Arcade, photographed in 1976.

The same room as above on 31 June 1978.

The carpets were situated on the ground floor of the Cabinet building, photographed in 1976.

In 1978 the carpet department was on the first floor of the middle building.

The coat department on the first floor of The Hayes building in 1976.

The linen department was on the first floor of the middle building, photographed in 1977.

The gift department on the second floor of The Hayes building in May 1978. Compare it with the photograph at the bottom of page 118.

In 1977 the materials were on the first floor of the middle building.

Special Occasions

The wedding reception of Mena and Ken Spencer was held in the Oak Room at the store on 26 July 1948.

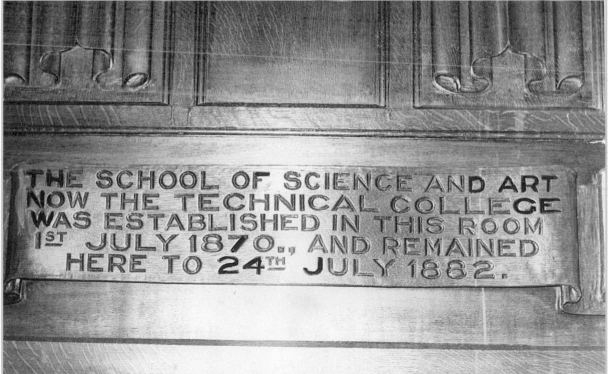

The plaque, which stood over the fireplace in the Oak Room, reveals a little bit of history. This was the precursor of University College, Cardiff

The 1958 January sales, and the lady in the top photograph clearly didn't want her picture taken. Shop walker Bert Mantle is welcoming the customers.

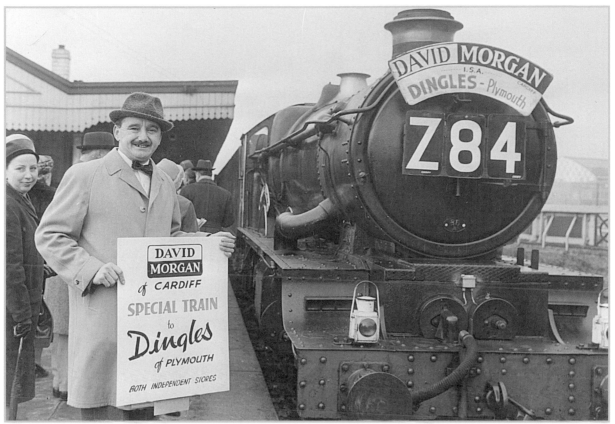

On 19 March 1963 the company laid on a special train from Cardiff to Dingles of Plymouth. Here is publicity manager G. Jayne Rees. The purpose of the visit was to learn from Dingles and compare methods. Dingles was independent then.

Front row, left to right: Gerald Morgan, G. Jayne Rees, Bobby Hall, Trevil Morgan, Miss Robbins, Muriel James and Molly and Bert Needham.

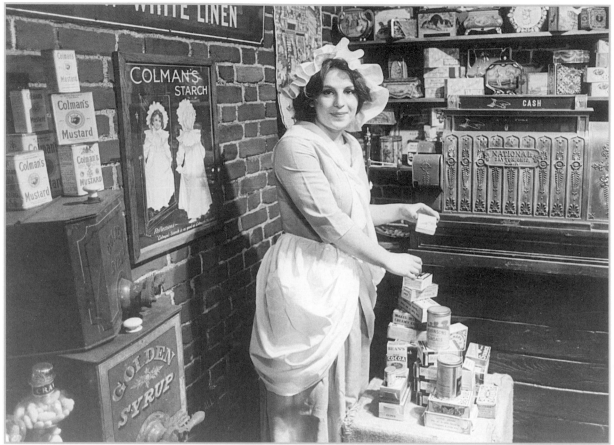

David Morgan centenary celebrations exhibits in 1979. In the top picture Sian Gaze, 22, takes a step back in time.

The centenary exhibition was placed here because it was two floors above the original shop on The Hayes. Compare it with the picture at the bottom of page 113.

Some more pictures of the David Morgan centenary celebrations exhibits. The cobblestone road looks so real. The two girls were from Lloyds Bank, High Street. Lloyds ran a feature on David Morgan Ltd in their national house magazine to mark that they had banked at the same branch since 1879.

Managing director John Morgan presents a cheque for £2,000 to the Scout Post in December 1987.

A cooking demonstration during the centenary celebrations of 1979.

David Morgan's '88 years of progress' float in 1968.

Pictured in front of the old display stockroom and grotto, known as 'the cathedral', which was due to be demolished in 1993, is Gloria Thornburn, publicity controller and a former display assistant.

'That's the way to do it.' Pancake Day in 1974.

A winning smile: Sarah Giardano takes the lead in the David Morgan charity pancake race in 1988.

The new middle building escalator is completed, and managing director John Morgan joins workers in a celebratory drink in 1979.

John Turner (left) and John Morgan studying renovation plans for the south building escalator, spring 1988. It was opened by Peter Walker, see page 78.

'Everything is going according to plan.' The installation of the south building escalator in 1988.

David Morgan staff with a cheque made out for £2,000 to the Meningitis Trust in 1988. Back row, left to right: Ann, name unknown, Marion Walker, Pat Atkins, Helen Boland. Front row: Ossie Dollah, Sian Holland, Catherine Porch, name unknown, name unknown.

The winners of the 'Barry in Bloom' competition with their certificates at the presentation party, with Gloria Thorburn, publicity controller.

Phil Dando's Jazz Band at a David Morgan gala evening in 2001.

A double bass world record attempt in November 2000.

Happy faces at a David Morgan staff dance held in the Whitehall Room, Park Hotel, *c*.1936.

This picture was taken on the roof of the store in 1939 and shows some of the staff members who joined the RAF. Among them are Reg Tarr, Bill Gaskin and Stan Davies, dressed in a suit.

The actor in uniform is television star Michael Aspel. He is pictured with other members of the cast of the David Morgan drama group, The Hayes Players, in a performance of *The Paragon*. Aspel was an employee at the time, in 1954.

Jackie Thomas and Rhiannon Harries try out the new escalator in 1993.

The Lord Lieutenant of South Glamorgan, Captain Norman Lloyd-Evans, who opened the new Bakers Row building on 28 October 1993, the 160th anniversary of the birth of David Morgan.

The David Morgan 'glamour girls' at a gala night in 1988.

This young lady won vouchers in the 1999 David Morgan 'Passion for Fashion' competition. Managing director David Lloyd is on the left of the picture.

Managing director John Morgan is seen here with members of the Cardiff Harlequins Rugby Club, who were sponsored by the firm, in 1989.

A regular customer of the Oak Room restaurant was Cyril Waite who always sat in the same place under a collage of a cello player, which he had admired. Director Richard Morgan got to hear about it and presented it to him. The girls on the right are Maggs, Mary and Marian.

Over the years, fashion parades were a regular feature in the store, this one taking place in around 1963. This was in the top rank, which later became C&A.

Shop assistants, sisters Andera and Eileen Kitzinger, show their skills on the centenary evening on 31 October 1979.

David Morgan Ltd bought the above Penarth shop, Howell Bros., in 1959, and the bottom picture shows how it looked in May 1977. It was sold to Dan Evans of Barry in January 2004.

The Penarth staff of David Morgan Ltd donned red noses for Comic Relief in 1988. Manager Doreen Morgan with Rita Cross, Sheila Taunton, Molly Currall, Jan Williams, Audrey Jones, Mary Beard, Gwyneth Jones and Barbara Walker.

The original shop was in Pontlottyn and opened in 1858. This is a photograph of the first branch, in Abertillery, opened in 1875. It traded as 'The Pontlottyn Shop'. The shop was sold in early 1920 and the building is now a small supermarket.

The Hayes Sports Teams

David Morgan had several hockey and rugby teams at the turn of the century, and the well-dressed shop girls in this picture were members of The Hayes ladies hockey team.

Hayes (Cardiff) Junior Hockey Club, season 1910–11.

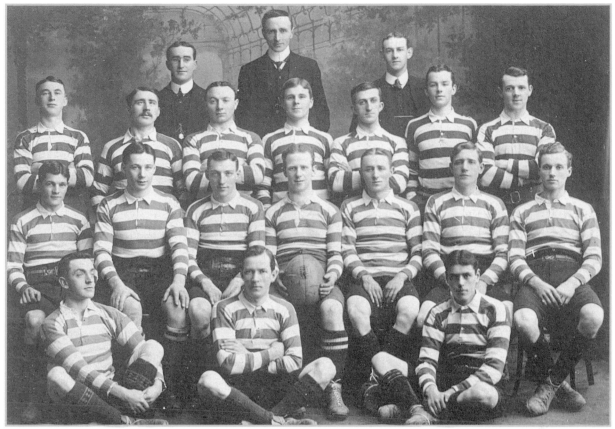

Hayes (Cardiff) Rugby Football Club, season 1908–9.

This postcard of the Hayes Hockey Club, season 1907–8, was addressed to a Miss Jackson of 14 St Mary Street, Cardiff, and posted in the city on 6 March 1908.

Hayes (Cardiff) Hockey Club, season 1909–10.

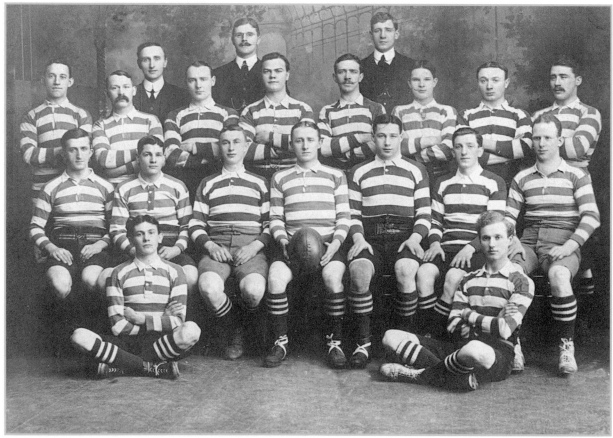

Hayes (Cardiff) Rugby Club, season 1909–10.

Long Service Dinner 2004

The David Morgan staff long service dinner was held in the store's 'Top of the Shop' restaurant. Martin Ford, Richard Angle and Alan Lowe sit opposite their wives, Ann, Becky and Sally.

Left to right: Julian Matthews, Pam Pearce, Mandy Matthews and Sandra Willett.

David (joint managing director) and Jan Andrews (front) share a table with Angela Hamilton and Estelle Ash.

May Sheers and Jan White give a nice smile for the photographer.

This happy couple are Nick and Janette Dodd.

Sandra Willett and Pam Pearce are all smiles.

James Shaughnessy and his wife, Helen.

Carol Williams and Eric Wakley after being presented with their David Morgan badges for 15 years service.

Yvonne Williams (wife of John Williams, merchandise director) and Shaun England.

These ladies worked in the underwear department. Left to right: Junc Phillips, Shirley Senior, Joan Dale, Muriel Stephens, Ann Llewellyn and Maureen Fitzgibbon. Ann Llewellyn completed 50 years with the company.

Keith Preston and Carol Kinsey.

Left to right: Meryl Phillips (director of services), Dolores Rich (retired fashion director) and John Morgan.

Some Members of Staff

David Morgan carpenter Arthur Dinham and his wife Celia both completed 50 years with the company.

Display manager Lynne Riby with her mannequins in 1992. The origin of mannequins dates to the 18th century when barbers used to have heads outside their shops and dressmakers used headless dummies on which to fit clothes.

Joint managing director Carol Kinsey in 2004.

Sue Jones, secretary to the managing director, in 2004.

James Shaughnessy, head of publicity, in 2004.

Janette Dodd, wages manager, in 2004.

Ruth Watton, personnel secretary, in 2004.

Assistants Ann Dobbins and Clair Mills in 2004.

Mike Thomas, graphic designer, in 2004.

Carol Williams, stock controller, in 2004.

June Larsen, credit control manager, in 2004.

Twins Sue and Carol Williams in 2004.

Gaynor Joseph and Meryl Phillips, director, in 2002.

Mary Baker and Pat Fishlock seen holding the 'top sales' cup in 2004.

John Llewellyn sold beds in the store for 22 years, pictured in 2002.

Mike Gorey sold furniture for 10 years, pictured in 2004.

Left to right: Maureen Fitzgibbon, Julie Carpenter, Mary Brown, Cheryl Durante, Ann Llewellyn, Joan Dale and Sharron Amey, pictured in 1999.

Assistants Linda Griffiths and Zena Gharibi in 2005.

Cellar Coffee Shop staff in 2004. Left to right: Mary Cullen, Sheridan Morgan and Jennifer Davies.

Cellar Coffee Shop staff Mairwen Ridout and Ria Holley in 2004.

James Mullins, furniture sales consultant, in 2004.

Shaun England, photographed *c.*1990, later became merchandise director.

Gordon Tinto, sales floor manager, in 2004.

John Williams, furniture buyer and later merchandise director, c.1990.

'Top of the Shop' restaurant staff in 2005. Left to right: Nigel Pepworth, catering manager, Mike Whitcombe, Heidi Stratten-Palmer, Brenda Jones and Margaret Cox.

These three ladies, Kathleen Hannay, Barbara Wayne and Beryl Harris, all worked in the store during the 1940s. When they retired they regularly met in David Morgan's for a cup of tea and a chat.

Mags O'Keefe, banking room cashier, in 2004.

Carpenter Rex Benson was on the David Morgan payroll for nearly 50 years, pictured in 2004.

Sharon Lord, Rachel Lord and Nerys Morgan preparing the store's 'a fragrance Christmas evening' in 2000.

Sheila Watkeys, Lewis Thomas and Betty Davis try out the new armchairs in the furniture department, *c.*2000.

Bob Sealey worked in the store during the 1980s.

Chris Rogers smiles for the photographer, Beatty French, who took many of the staff photographs in this book.

Some Memorable Moments

Preparing the Christmas puddings in 1963 are, left to right: Chef Reginald Wong, Chef Len Worcub, G. Jayne Rees (publicity manager) and Chef Harry McElligott who completed 50 years with the company.

Sir Geraint and Lady Brenda Evans arriving at the store for the centenary celebrations in 1979, met by smart commissionaire Ray Brown. Behind is group chairman David Morgan.

Mike Thomas and Paul Evans help to serve the drinks on a gala evening.

Meryl Phillips and Nigel Pepworth at a gala evening.

Staff on a weekend outing to Blackpool, *c.*1965.

Another staff outing, *c.*1965.

Tom Lloyd, Thelma and Ralph Cantlebury at a staff party, *c*.1960.

Another David Morgan staff party, *c*.1960.

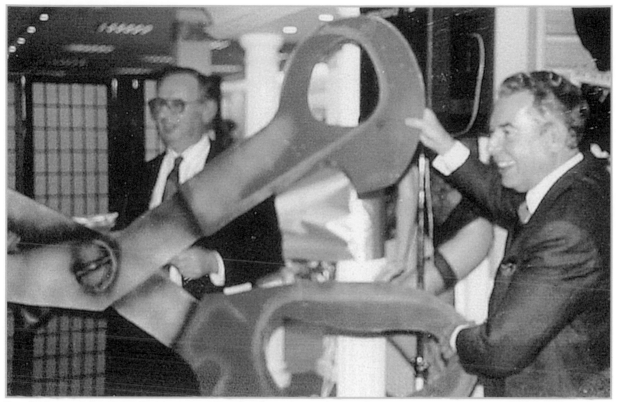

Lord Lieutenant Captain Norman Lloyd-Edwards performs the opening ceremony of the north atrium on 31 October 1993.

Susanne Burg of Deutschland Radio, the German Public Radio Service, interviewing James Shaughnessy, publicity manager, a few days before the closure of the store.

High jinks at the David
Morgan Christmas
party in 2002.

The Kayser princesses, Mary
Thomas (hosiery) and
Pamela Andrews (lingerie),
try on some high heeled
shoes on their special visit
to the store in 1960.

The Final Days

Father Christmas pays his last ever visit to the store in December 2004.

Even the polar bear in Santa's grotto looks sad.

The author took this picture of Nesta Thomas on the day of closing. Nesta visited the store six days a week for 20 years. She always arrived at 9am sharp and stayed until lunchtime. Known as the Queen of David Morgan Ltd, staff would bow to her as they passed.

Sean Kerr and Karan Lewis manage a closing day smile.

The shelves are bare, and Elena Evans, Sandra Davies and Ann Locke have nothing more to sell.

More bare shelves but plenty of smiles. Left to right: Pat Smith, Pat Atkins, June Hill, Marilyn Clarke, Craig Baker and Lydia Fitzsimmons.

Left to right: Elaine Thomas, Sally Ford, Marie Hamer, Hushnara Begum, Lisa Jenkins, Pat Smith, Pat Atkins and June Hill.

'Where did they get those hats?' Left to right: Keris Marsh, Dawn Jolies, Sandra Secome and Adelina Woodruff.

Left to right: Gareth McMahon, Sabina Begum, Marlene Harvard, Carol Nash and John Walters.

These two posters really say it all.

The popular Cellar Coffee Shop. Below, the author's wife, Jacqueline, enjoys her last cup of coffee on the day it closed. During the war, it was used as an air-raid shelter and many a romance is said to have flourished there.

Freelance photographer Roy Paul took some of the pictures featured in this chapter. Left to right: Christine Russ, Ann Dobbins, Helen Nolan, Maggie Cullinan, Daniel Hillier and Lynne Cuddihy.

Back, left to right:: Gareth McMahon, Claire Sanderson, Philip Davies, Sandra McIntyre, John Mills, Alan Lowe (buyer), Michael Struebig and Joanne McKenzie. Front, left to right: Christine Cowlin, Sandra Willett, Sabina Begum, Mary Jones, Melanie Evans and June Hart.

Smiling faces but sad hearts. Left to right: Philip Davies, Mary Havard, Margaret Cotterell, Carol Nash, Christine Cowlin, Gareth McMahon and Alan Lowe (buyer).

Melanie Evans, seen wearing the Red Indian head-dress, wrote a special song about the store, which was sung by staff and customers just before closing time. Left to right: Sandra Willett, Sabina Begum, John Mills, Mary Jones, June Hart, Alan Lowe, Barbara Morgan, Joan Addecott, Joan Holland, Olwen Jones and Liz Tyler.

The 'Top of the Shop' restaurant staff pose for a final picture. Left to right: Kelly Wang, Suzanne Hoole, Pauline Solomon, Mags Cox, Mary Cullen, Jenny Davies and Margaret Ridout.

Left to right: Sheridan Morgan, Helen Crane, Sue Williams and Brenda Jones.

'I'm in the mood for dancing'. Dot Doe and Theresa Jones.

'And it is goodbye from us.' Michelle Burnett and Nicola Young.

Melanie Evans gets everyone involved in her song.

Left to right: Carol Nash, Richard Barfoot, Gareth McMahon, Sandra Willett, Sandra McIntyre, Sabina Begum, Mary Jones and Alan Lowe.

Shoe and boot repairer Geraint Searle stands alongside a poster which reads, 'We are closed. We have a shop on St Mary Street.'

A sombre looking stock control clerk, Ceri Twohey.

'What a day to celebrate my 60th birthday', sighs Sandra Willett, photographed with Phil Davies.

'And it is goodbye from them.' Andrew White, Janet Jacklin and Alan Jones.

This lady, who has shopped in the store for many years, has a last cuppa in the 'Top of the Shop' restaurant.

Phyllis O'Connell, a David Morgan Ltd customer since 1947, just cannot believe the store is closing.

These David Morgan badges, which were on sale for just £3, are sure to become collectors' items.

Even the sweepings went for 10 pence a bag.

The rush before 5pm for the last-minute bargains.

Staff and customers sing *Auld Lang Syne*.

The clock strikes five and David Morgan Ltd closes its doors to shoppers for the final time.

Gareth McMahon closes the door for the last time.

The Wake

The night of the store's closure, on 29 January 2005, David Morgan Ltd had a wake in the basement for the staff. The following group pictures were taken by graphic designer Mike Thomas.

David Morgan Ltd customers will miss seeing all these staff members, who were a credit to the company over the years.

The menswear department. Seated in the centre on the front row is buyer Alan Lowe. There are also cardboard cut-outs of John Morgan and Richard Morgan at the back of the picture.

Mr. John & Mr. Richard
Goodbye and
thank you for everything.
From everyone at
David Morgan

'And it is goodbye from all of us.'

The administration staff who worked on the fourth floor of the building. Back, left to right: Sarah Wardrobe, Carol Williams, James Shaughnessy, Beatty French, Janette Dodd and Sarah Wells. Front, left to right: Richard Morgan-Isaac, Sally Parker, Mags O'Keefe, Christine Rogers, Ruth Watton, Jan White and Daniel Chapple.

The electrical department. Seated in the centre on the front row is buyer Richard Angle. Back, left to right: David Hornso-Pedersen, Graham Williams, Jason Butler, Rhys Lewis, Chris Chandler and John Trezise. Front, left to right: David Scurlock, Adam Thomas, Richard Angle, Michael Williams and Ian Gunn.